The element, carbon,]
Poyser's life. He comes
roots deep in the are.   .... Nottinghamshire
coalfields and his natal village of Mansfield
Woodhouse. His university studies at South
Kensington's Imperial College of Science and
Technology led to a career in organic chemistry (the
myriad compounds of carbon), whilst retirement from
the pharmaceutical industry in 2007 saw a move to
organic gardening and the flourishing of his lifelong
love of poetry: a primrose path from C-reactive protein
to C-reative Writing, so to speak. No coincidence then
that he's a member of Macclesfield Creative Writing
Group and an active open-miker in and around the
North-West.

Since publishing "Eric Bloodaxe? And Other Verse" in
2014, he has been trawling his archives and furiously
writing to bring together the present collection which
takes its impetus, title and 8 of its 60 poems (not
counting those in Injury Time) from his family, past
and present.

He lives in Macclesfield with Mady and, in addition to
writing, bridge playing and growing vegetables, cycles a
bit.

Website: doggerelbanksy.wordpress.com

Praise for Seconds Out

"Thought-provoking, poignant and amusing by turn, Phil Poyser visits themes as diverse as DIY and the Parfitt Drive Penguin. This collection is a romp and a delight."

- Joy Winkler, author of "Town" and "Stolen Rowan Berries".

"This second collection from Phil Poyser is in essence a compendium; something for everyone. Phil writes with consummate wit in 'Notice Board', tells of parental love, of give and take in, 'Character Four' and 'Injury Time 1914', says everything you need to know with scarcity of words.

A collection to read and then read again."

- Margaret Holbrook, author of "Picking the Bones".

SECONDS OUT

BY
PHIL POYSER

For
Paula
and for
Mike and Rachel,
Samuel, Maxim and Alex
Also in memory of
my brother, Alan,
who died 25/09/2009
et
aussi dédié à mes beaux-frères:
Léon (Léo) Jouglet, décédé le 26/09/2013
et Marcel Langlais, décédé le 25/03/2009
Vous nous manquez tous les deux.

Retirement walk, 2007, in the Rhinogs with the
ironically named Real Men's Club.

The author with sister, Jean, early 1950's.

Contents

Injury Time

Seconds Out

He'd fought most of the big names in his day, our Dad:
middle weights, Terry Spinks, Chris Eubanks;
light heavies, Randolph Turpin, Don Cockell;
and the serious stuff, Rocky Marciano, Henry Cooper,
Cassius Clay (as he then was).

I'm watching him as he watches the boxing
from his ringside seat in front of the TV,
ducking and weaving, shoulders twitching,
as he swings, first a right (he was a southpaw, Pa)
and a left, a jab, a feint, then working the body
with a punishing combination of punches,
before rocking back with the deftness of Muhammad
Ali,
floating out of range of flailing fists.

When the bell rings to end the round,
he sits back, drained from the effort,
and prepares for Round 2.
He's up on points, but it's early days.
Mam fusses over him, as he crouches on the stool,
making sure his gum shield is out,
giving him water to spit into the bucket,
orange segment, towel for his brow.
Gum shield at the ready, she whispers advice into his
ear,
taking the teacup from his outstretched hand.

The bell. Seconds out. Round 2.

Love Actually: For Mady

The theme is "Love" and so I'm spurred
to write in haste these lines absurd,
expressing how, when first we met,
some astral signs must have occurred.

How in the dusky sky a jet
left vapour trail, no Exocet*,
but just a line across the night,
awaiting, incomplete as yet.

Then from the East, in failing light,
conditions by good luck just right,
to thus complete a random X,
there came at last another flight.

That kiss was prelude to the pecks
bestowed on cheeks, and later, necks.
By twenty years the rest is blurred,
my Love, and varifocal specs.

"exocet" is French for "flying fish"

Valentine Limerick

There once was a cherub called Cupid
fired arrows. That's what I call stupid.
Just to do it was crass,
but they're fired from his ass:
no bow, so he saved quite a few quid.

Lunch Chez Simone (and Léo)

It's summer, a day or so after the first squall.
The trestle table nestles invitingly in the shadow
and we are preparing for lunch *al fresco*.
A buzz of expectation excites the adolescent flies.
Storm water has gathered in the crevices of the four
white, plastic chairs,
stacked, legs beseeching skywards.

One by one, the chairs are righted and wiped,
sun-dried briefly and positioned along the table,
looking out over lawn and away
to the meadow and tree-lined stream beyond.
There is a chair for each of us
and one to spare...

After lunch, we sit and chat,
update a year gone by,
reminisce, dust off mottled anecdotes
and vaguely note their subtle, time-wrought evolution.
Close by, your absence fills the fourth chair.
A shiver of wind ruffles the cloth.

You get up, smooth it down,
nod, offer more wine,
walk round the table,
share a joke, chuckle
and are gone once more.

Casey's Gate

I've written poems on gardening themes:
there's "Eric Bloodaxe?", lost in dreams;
there's one I called "Allotment Dawn";
one cursed why cabbage whites were born;
another told when frenzied dash
for horse manure caused quite a clash;
and skits: "Chard of the Brookfield Spade";
"Just One Courgetto" serenade;
and Guy "Forks" night in 2010.
Blow me! It's time to write again.

"The reason is," I hear him say,
in soothing burr from Gloucester way,
"it wun't be right to quite ignore
the fact. That's wha' you poets are for."
So, let me tell you of the state
that's led to Casey's brand new gate.

The one we had with chain and lock
the slightest breeze would shake and rock.
Its fragile structure so vibrated,
replacement was investigated.
Cometh the hour, cometh the man.
T'Committee formed a cunning plan.

"That gate will fall on some young kid."
Prophetic words. It almost did.
So urgent action was required
by someone overall attired.
They scratched their heads. "Who could it be?"
In unison, they cried, "Casey."

To Casey they then turned to ask
if he'd take on this mammoth task.
He thought a second, then replied,
"Your faith in me can't be denied.
I'll do it, friends. Leave it to me
and we shall see what we shall see."

The next weekend, it scarcely rained.
A certain man the gate unchained,
from trusty van his tools removed,
laid out his plan, as is approved
and noted distances and angles,
once his tape measure disentangles.

With knitted brows and maledictions,
he calculated space restrictions,
marked out where the gate would swing
by using lengths of twine and string.
All that remained in line of duty?
Arrange delivery of the beauty.

Two stalwart wooden posts were bought,
essential items to support
the metal framework and the grill.
The treasurer asked to see the bill,
paled visibly and clutched his chest,
a deep sigh heaved, "Well, you know best."

So Casey delved, then dug some more.
Great mounds of soil upon the floor
rose up towards the hills and sky
and stood at least 2 metres high.
Cement was bought. Cement was mixed,
poured into holes and posts affixed.

On 25th. of Jan. was hung
the gate whose praises I have sung.
On top and on each side stood proud
that grill to stop those not allowed
from climbing over, breaking in.
Job done! My, didn't our Casey grin!

So, gone old, rickety disgrace,
a spanking new one in its place.
All that remains (the fame is his):
to christen "Casey's Gate" with fizz.

Notice Board

At home we have a notice board
to plan the coming weeks.
There's loads of stuff still gets ignored:
pay milk; 'phone Jim; plant leeks.

We use it as a memory aid,
so social whirl survives.
Then once it's past the date displayed,
we wipe away our lives.

The list begins "Defrost the fridge";
"Canaries: book the flight";
"Wednesday at Mike and Claire's for bridge".
(My God! Is that tonight?)

Some items simply pass me by.
Sometimes I need my specs.
Today, an entry grabbed my eye:
"The Snow Goose, Tuesday, Sex."

Beverage Almond Gnawwood Cleansetail

Our hamster's in an awful rage.
She sits and fumes inside her cage.
She thinks this time we've gone too far,
our furry prisoner at the bar.

For every evening on the dot
she exercises on the plot
comprised of landing, hall and stairs,
pausing to groom beneath the chairs.

It's then she leaves her fur-lined nest
(about the time we get undressed),
her ears erect, her nose a-twitch,
(but first to soothe that nagging itch.)

From time to time, we have a scare.
We glance away. She isn't there.
For hours we scour the kitchen round,
anxious for the slightest sound.

If, like tonight, we are not there,
she'll stare and think or simply stare,
or pull and tug her tatty cover,
yearn wistfully for hamster lover.

Some days she doesn't sleep too well.
We're noisy neighbours sent from Hell,
diurnal strange insomniacs
who wait for night-time to relax.

A self-respecting vertebrate
knows when it's time to activate,
once sun has dipped and darkness falls
and shadows steal along the walls.

By day she dreams a cunning plan
for Rodent victory over Man:
draw up petition which with paw would
be marked Cleansetail, Beverage Gnawwood;

or (unhinged, alone and barmy)
Hamster Liberation Army,
with Foxy beret à la Che
or balaclava (IRA),

sit on haunches, raise clenched paw.
Today the hall. Tonight the door.
Tomorrow, so her reasoning goes,
...a noise disturbs rebellious doze...

...go placard-waving down the street:
GIVE EVERY HAMSTER MORE TO EAT;
LET'S TURN THE TABLES, NOT THE WHEEL;
MINIMUM CHOW IS ONE SQUARE MEAL.

WE WON'T WAIT FOR EVOLUTION.
THE PET SHOP GIRLS WANT REVOLUTION;
STOP CHANGING CAGES TWICE A WEEK.
A LIBERTY? A BLOODY CHEEK.

But then again, all snug and warm,
she sees the case for slow reform
and, as she slips back into trance,
decides to give us one more chance.

Barnacle Geese: On a Wing and a Prayer

The voice is unmistakable:
warm; caring; thoughtful; knowledgeable.
The voice-over caresses the viewer,
pied-pipers us into the real world of Life or Death:
survival of the fittest or of the most fortunate?
That tilt of the head, the eyes, that tuft of rebellious hair,
immediately identifiable: indefatigable;
eternal as the earth around us;
committed; yet non-judgemental; indestructible.
And Life is harsh, yet resilient...

unlike the little fluff bundles.
We see them hatch in their "eryie",
atop a sky-high rock stump,
teetering above the scree, and two days later,
watch them leap into the void
or slide rather, slip, tumble, stumble,
trip, fall and, yes, leap,
and then it's a gravitational lottery,
an air resistance, terminal velocity,
a ping pong, pin ball, bagatelle.
We imagine the scores ratcheting up:
100, 200, 250, 400...
At last, the scree slope. Then all is still.
Game over.

Mum and Dad Barnacle Goose honk their approval,
and, miraculously, of the five goslings,
first one, then two and finally three,
somehow shake the scree dust from their proto-
feathers
to waddle dazedly towards the sea,
where they slip into that soothing parental wake,
ready for the next step,
the next great leap forward,
the next leap into the unknown.

First Tattoo

I bit the bullet and got my first today.
It didn't hurt – much – just a few pricks, tiny bites
of the needle. "Like a blood sugar test,"
she said sweetly, the sympathetic professional.
Amongst the waiting crowds, young people,
more than I would have expected
and some of them regulars,
sporting frothy, feathered tangles of
primary-coloured exotica on forearms,
a Chinese philosopher's enigmatic pictogram
or, unknowingly, a menu item,
like a footballer or the "Illustrated Man,"
some with necks declaring heavy metal allegiance:
Motörhead, Black Sabbath, Iron Maiden.
Others, more discrete David Dimblebys,
a senior moment of indiscretion tucked away
above a scapula, on a hip or between
the umbilicus and the mound of Venus,
a cynical arrow from Cupid's bow,
"This way to the pleasure palace."

Now there's a sea shanty running through my mind:
"What shall we do with a drunken sailor,
earl-y in the morning?"
L O V E - H A T E on the knuckles; Mother;
a snake-coiled rose; the current girl in every port.

It's not always been the rage, of course,
the must have fashion accessory,
defiant two fingers to society's conformists.
Once upon a time and long, long ago
when I was a little boy,
 it was a reminder on the living to the living
of Life's lottery, the guilt of survival,
when so many, so very many, perished;
still legible on the parchment skin
their transformation to nameless number.

Christie Bell

With hands clasped on chest and fingers intertwined,
I'm stretched out, head on block, waiting,
transfixed in stone or bronze,
a petrified medieval knight or bishop,
and it's definitely not my move.
Feet slightly apart, haunches tweaked into position,
adjustments made to the millimetre, I'm ready.
A sudden exodus as the otherwise attentive staff
scurry to observe from the safety of the next room
and, as the lights dim,
I'm alone with the machine.

It whirrs a greeting, as if slightly annoyed,
does as it has been told to do,
zaps, circumnavigates my rigid pelvis,
fires again, three times in all.
There is background music, scratchy, sub-audible,
but it should be loud, incongruous, "The Blue
Danube,"
a lilting waltz for this egocentric odyssey.
Lights back on and everyone's brisk and jolly.
It's the last session, so time to ring the corridor bell,
and without asking for whom,
announce to the world, to the waiting rooms
that I'm in the zap of the gods.

Myth

I went to see a shaman whose reputation's great.
He had a magic potion to stop me being late.
It stung a bit. It stank a lot. It really tasted foul.
The shaman's grin was rather smug. He looked like
Simon Cowell.
I grimaced and I spluttered and I felt that I would
choke
and then I made to shrug it off, 'cos I'm that kind of
bloke.
So now, my friends, my lateness past has joined the
realm of myth.
Last week I came here early. That's the truth. I claim
the Fifth.

One Bill Bill Didn't Push Through Congress or *Clintoris Monicae*

Congress is sitting ; Monica's kneeling.
The President's standing, senses reeling.
He concentrates on the Oval orifice,
anything, Lord, but that rhythmical kiss.
The struggle's vain - those lips of Monica's! -
She knows he knows she wears no knickers.
"God bless Uummm-er-i-ca! God bless! God bless!
Oh God…!
                    Of course this doesn't count as
congress.
That's swell. Same time, same place, next week, I
guess?
Naturally, I'll pay for laundering the dress."
(Ironically, he's paying for not laundering the dress!)

Act of   A   Random Kindness

bo
dy
flo
ats
in the
H udson
Ri v e r.
A little boy's
body   floats
in the river,
comes ashore
f r o m   t h e
Hudson River,
nudged ashore on
Manhattan   Island.
Amorphous   shape
that's washed ashore,
anonymous   form
that can't be named,
lost overboard or
slipped in the river,
swimming alone and
the current too strong ?
Missed by no-one ?
No-one comes forward.
A child has gone missing
and   no-one   knows.
But a random death
should not be forgotten.
And New Yorkers act,
a knee-jerk response.
"Don't be a jerk. Give
a dime. Give a quarter."
And quarter is given,
a   reflex   response.
For a random death
should not go forgotten.

From public subscription, a random response, a little white
monument soon is erected, lost in the woods in Riverside Park,
marking the spot where the child came ashore, marking
the spot in the heart of New Yorkers, "Which no-one expects,"
our Tour Guide confided. The   phrase   he   shared
with   us,   like   a   Hearst-coined   front   pager.
"ACT OF RANDOM KINDNESS   :   VERY FEW HURT."

The Sun Shone down All Day

After the harvester had passed
and ripened sheaves of corn been stacked,
we'd head into those spaces vast,
those prairies with adventures packed
and play and play and play and play,
back where the sun shone down all day.
Inside our wigwams, brave and squaw
would share what frugal fare we had,
whilst cavalry prepared for war
and in the nick of time came Dad.
No powwow needed down our way,
back where the sun shone down all day.

The Great White Chief spoke. We obeyed.
Time to go with resignation,
yet feeling we had been betrayed,
confined within our reservation,
confined until first morning's ray,
back where the sun shone down all day.
Those days stretched on without an end
like buffalo upon the plain.
Each with the next would blur and blend,
a shifting, disappearing train
we're on. Oh, but we'd have loved to stay
back where the sun shone down all day.

For all too soon, just like the corn,
we changed, grew up. We aged, matured.
The sun still rose and shone at dawn,
but we from childhood's play were lured.
And now the skies at times are grey
where once the sun shone down all day.

The D-I-Y Whodunnit? Not Me.

It's weird. The "Marie Celeste" was unmanned,
adrift and abandoned so far from the land,
but there's one side of Life where I'm all at sea
which I'm happy to share as it's no mystery.

It's the one that requires a handyman's skill
and for its devotees is run-of-the-mill.
My "Doing-It-Yourself" is just D-I-Y hell.
It makes me ill-tempered. I shout and I yell.

A tap that is dripping, a fuse that has blown,
straightway I'm in territory unknown.
I don't have the tools, the ones that I need
and any instructions, impossible to read.

They're written by aliens to bamboozle me.
I'm a D-I-Y I-D-I-O- and -T.
My screwdriver's not Phillips®. For me, that's Hi-Fi.
Why B 'n' Q? Why S 'n' M? Why D-I-Y?

A jigsaw's a puzzle. I don't know the drill.
Sanding a surface doesn't give me a thrill.
The thought of that thought and pre-preparation
fills me with panic and mild palpitation.

One Truth fundamental, take it as read.
D-I-Y, my, oh, my, it does in my head.
Decorating a room or installing a shelf?
Pay someone to do it. Won't Do-It-Myself.

UKIP: Nightmare in Westminster

Last night I had the strangest dream:
UKIP had been elected,
continuing their head of steam.
In droves voters defected.

But as the Chamber filled again,
it must have been a mirage:
just four MPs and all were men
and none was Nigel Farage.

No cries of "Shame!" were echoing round,
no braying, "Mr. Speaker,"
just Big Ben's clock the only sound
and this was growing weaker.

No Cameron, no Miliband,
there was no Clegg to stand on,
the House of Commons undermanned,
in green, cross-benched abandon,

whilst upstairs in another place
where they had been up-Lorded
to stop these worthies losing face
(which none of us applauded)

these Lords were slumped and only stirred,
their hect'ring ways retaining,
when "Cash for questions" time occurred
(brown envelopes pertaining.)

For then they cobwebs brushed aside,
became so animated,
Time's whirring hands each one defied
and through the night debated.

"Keep Britain ours. Keep Britain for
the wealthy and the land rich.
These immigrants oust home grown poor."
Ed choked on bacon sandwich.

Meanwhile the country soldiered on,
notched in its belts of leather.
"It's just the way we told you, son,
we're all in this together.

We're in it for the medium term
and in it for the long haul.
The public must with us stand firm
or economy will stall."

The chimes of midnight New Year's Eve
disturbed my anxious dreaming.
What I had seen was make believe,
but it still had me screaming.

So when in May it's time to vote
with evenings long and balmy,
don't make the English Channel moat.
Avoid UKIP tsunami.

The Music of the Warriors: [1]

Had Hitler played the banjo and Goebbels ukulele
and had they had a strumming practice session daily,
they might have spared us all the pain of fighting World War II
and concentrated on careers entertaining me and you.
I'm thinking, "Battling Banjos", George Formby's gormless grin.
Perhaps they'd have invited as guest singer, Vera Lynn.
Alas, they spent their days as hatred-spouting demagogues,
defining Master races, them *v* us, the underdogs.

If Napoleon had played triangle and Josephine the harp,
they might have made sweet music and we couldn't really carp.
He'd have kept his little instrument tucked inside his coat
and on off days he'd say, "Pas ce soir, chérie" (quote, unquote).
And she'd be left to play her plangent harp tunes solitaire,
whilst from Moscow he retreated mauled by that Russian bear.
"Able was I ere I saw Elbow," then to St Helena.
Moral: Stick to your bicornes and triangles. No brainer!

Attila was a lonely man despite attendant horde,
but had he played piano or struck a harpsichord,
he wouldn't have attacked the Roman Empire with the Hun.
His name would not strike fear nor be a concept that we shun,

his horsemanship as nothing to his playing a sonata.
Flash forward seven hundred years to Genghis Khan the Tatar.
If Genghis had played lead guitar for "The Mongols" metal band,
he would have spent less time migrating west across the sand.

If Ivan the Terrible had just practised that bit more,
he'd have improved and been Ivan the Moderately Poor.
His skill on the harmonica rivalling Larry Adler,
the Tsar of All the Russias' power would dominate and straddle her.
It might have soothed the troubled mind of Ivan the Unstable.
He might not have killed his son and been Ivan the Formidable.
With many wives, like the contemporaneous Henry VIII,
our Ivan had a sex drive that was difficult to sate.

We've spent some time imagining how music could have spared us
a blood stained history of atrocities and murders.
"For if music be the food of love, give me excess of it."
Will Shakespeare knew his madrigals though plays were what he writ.
"Music gives a soul to the universe and wings to the mind,"[2]
even those sad ones like me tone deaf, tone dumb, tone blind.
Remember though you feel it's just cacophony and dins,
it's also poetry. Where words leave off, music begins.[3]

[1]Thanks to Richard Sykes (Bollington, Cheshire, 30th. January, 2015) for the original idea.
[2] attributed to Plato
[3] Heinrich Heine

Poem 2 N4 (U, Chess 4 U)

TXTin x 3
DR **NA**1
U R in the Fucha.
owz@ sucha?
I am longon.
U R 2 cum.
In sum,
bummer 4 me,
kool 4 U.

lisN 2 me
& U will C.
Njoy ya time,
Mploy ya time.
B haP
B4 U R like me,
a lontime ded.
inuf sed.
TXTin x 3

Lady with Boy and Parasol

You'll know the painting that I mean.
Is it by Monet or Manet?
It's in a meadow, quiet, serene:
one of the Impressionists, anyway.
The lady's skirts just swish the grass.
Her parasol gives shade enough.
She twirls it gently as I pass.
I feel her bustle brush and scuff
the poppies. Ah, those blobs of red,
ephemeral, they will not last –
except on canvas. Shake your head
and sigh for future, present and the past.

Pigments of the Imagination

A little distance behind,
at the brow of the poppy field
is another mother and child, but no parasol.
The child may be younger and not able to keep up
with the bigger boy in the foreground.
The women could be sisters, sisters-in-law,
friends, neighbours or from the same village
or perhaps just necessary for balance,
shadows wandering onto the canvas
from the edge of Monet's mind.

Nine Men's Mudguard

In the run up to Christmas, some weeks ago,
on an overcast Wednesday, threat'ning to snow,
nine Broken Cross cyclists set out in a bunch
for Poplar 2000, that day's choice for lunch.
As always, hunched over, Phil had on his back
his worldly possessions crammed in his rucksack.
Sticking out of the top, so it spoiled the surprise,
a much needed mudguard to comments gave rise.

For weeks, months, no, years, rainy Wednesdays he'd
missed.
No mudguards made Phil a fair-weather cyclist.
If it came on to rain, alone in the crowd,
no-one rode behind him. The spray formed a cloud.
At last he decided, though it might be hard,
a fit day had arrived to fit that mudguard,
thrown in with the bike he'd bought from Mike Naden
who'd thus helped to make Phil's wallet less laden.

Now just beyond Boden, a red-mist arose
as a red-beret-'d hag got right up Phil's nose.
She honked, overtook and turned left with a glower.
"You were riding in twos at 10 miles an hour."
Phil jumped off his bike and confronted the crone
"You don't own the road," he seethed, his cool now
blown.
He didn't admit that – well, what could he say –
they hadn't gone that fast the whole of that day.

The harridan-witch from discussion declined,
Phil rejoined the group, mudguards back on his mind.
A soothing rest taken at Lavender Farm
soon helped to restore Phil's habitual calm.
At Poplar 2000, the lunch break complete,
nine intrepid cyclists got back on their feet.
John now suggested there was no better time
to mount the back mudguard. Cue: sheer pantomime.

Phil and John started. They were soon joined by Mick.
Six helpful onlookers chimed, "Come on. Be quick."
Out came the tools and with each one a remark.
Six voices in chorus said, "By four it's dark."
So nuts were removed and packing provided.
On *modus op'randi* views were divided.
One last turn of the screw and Mick gave a grunt.
A good job well done, so next week it's the front.

So Phil brought the mudguard and John picked the time
and Mick did a neat piece of "plumbing" sublime
and the chorus of 6 all helped to a man:
that's Jim, Bill, Roger, Dave, Dave and Stan.
So, how many cyclists to fit a mudguard?
"Phil, John, Mick and six comes to nine," says the bard.
That's how Nine Men's Mudguard came to be there
with Morris Men dancing it in Macc town square.

Et in Acadia We Go

Where emerald duckweed carpets and water hyacinths
entwine
and bayous choke if propagation's not limited with
brine,
"The Mysteries of the Swamp" tour has its latest group
on board,
out to see swamp creatures and leave no corner
unexplored.

When the alligator wakes and spies the tourists in a
bunch,
he stirs himself a little. (You can see he's thinking,
"Lunch".)
He slides into the water and skims across the bog.
(Unless you're really wide awake, you see a drifting log.)
Just eyes and nostrils visible, as silent as the grave,
relentlessly, he gathers speed, a saurian tidal-wave.

Though tourist fare it is at first fires his interest as a
goal,
he'll consider any morsel which he can swallow whole.
The cunning Cajun captain whets the 'gator's appetite
with tempting, white **marsh**mallow cubes, gone in a
single bite.
The jaws unclench and with his head he gives a
sideways roll.
Unblinkingly, he's back for more, sends shivers through
your soul,
for if he could but get you in the bayou by you'self,
there'd be no need for sweeties lifted from the grocer's
shelf.

Meanwhile, he'll jump for chicken dangled from a rod and line,
as shutters snap and tourists gasp to see this 'gator dine.
But the cunning Cajun captain still has one more surprise,
an eighteen inch pet 'gator who when stroked will close his eyes,
just hold him and caress him though you mustn't squeeze too hard
for though he's never bitten, you must stay upon your guard.

Then it's time to leave the swarms of lovebugs paired in in-flight bliss,
past cypress wading in melancholy symbiosis
with lank dank drapes of Spanish moss, past egrets monopod,
to meet again the 'gators when you tour the Land of Nod.

Misheard Bible Stories Retold:
1. Joshua and the Bottle of Sherry-O

When Joshua round a city was encamped,
his trumpets blew and his folk loudly stamped.
The walls fell down, the effect of stereo.
Joshua won a bottle of sherry-O.

Poem One: Start as You Mean to Go On

The covers are off. The lid's been removed.
Iambic pentameter's been approved.
First day of Jan., and I'm raring to go
when all of a sudden I stop in mid-flow.
I'm right on the brink of writing "Poem One",
but, look, it's couplets I've stumbled upon.
I'd made up my mind to write in blank verse,
to sweep away rhymes, such endings disperse.
New Year's resolutions made yesterday
abandoned in tatters, it's always the way.
I'd so looked forward to starting anew.
I'm deleting Poem One. On to Poem Two…

Misheard Bible Stories Retold:
2. Damson and Dee Lilacs

Der once was a strong kid called Damson,
whose 6 pack made him look damn handsome.
His girlfriend, Dee Lilacs,
his locks she like hijacks
for which she was paid a king's ransom.

Now, Damson, he was not best pleased,
more like he's completely off cheesed.
"I'm fed up with wimmin
hair sneakily trimmin'",
so brought the house down when he squeezed.

Misheard Bible Stories Retold:
3. The Animals Came in 4 x 4

God got fed up of human kind,
to partying they were much inclined.
He thought destroying with a flood
would do the world no end of good.

He got in touch with his mate, Noah,
on some kind of mystic blower.
He warned him of impending doom,
that rains will come and murk and gloom.

He said to Noah, "Build an ark,
your kin and animals embark."
So snakes that hiss and lions that roar,
Noah drove aboard in 4 x 4.

The cat and mouse, ant and aardvark
begrudgingly lived in the ark.
They all thus somehow co-abided
until the floods at last subsided.

The unicorn, he missed the boat
and sadly knew not how to float.
His like we shall not see again.
God sometimes wishes it were men.

Misheard Bible Stories Retold:
4. The Wisden of Solomon

Now there once reigned a very clever king
whose problem-solving was his special thing.
Less well known was his role in writing up
all test and county scores and cricket cup.
Overs, wickets, stands, every run that's scored,
all matches taking place at home, abroad,
for all posterity would be notated,
the Wisden of Solomon widely fêted.

The Chester Road Chimpanzee

There's a chimpanzee living in Chester Road.
He's arrived from The Congo. His new abode
is right at the top of a horse chestnut tree,
curious lodgings for a lone chimpanzee.
He doesn't look happy up there in his nest.
He sits there all day with his chin on his chest.
Perhaps it's our weather, skies cloudy and grey.
He'll acclimatise soon. It's like that our way.

Perhaps he is missing his loved ones and kin,
but he shouldn't let that get under his skin.
There's lots here to smile for: bananas in hands;
(There's Fair Trade® and Value® and other such
brands.)
monkey nuts; ape-ricots; and orange-utans.
They surely will help him with homesickness pangs
and we'll coax him down with his favourite tea.
But is that Br-Brook Bond® or tips of PG®?

The Parfitt Drive Penguin

There's a p-p-p-penguin in Parfitt Drive.
He simply appeared. No one saw him arrive.
No one can decide where he sources his fish.
He seems to have access to all he could wish.
He stands like a statue by our neighbours' ponds.
Perhaps it's their goldfish with which he absconds:
one minute beak empty, his wings by his side,
the next waddles off as if he's satisfied,
work done, shift over, so back home to the wife.
I swear that he's thinking that this is the Life.

The down side is that Farnsfield weather is grim,
practically sub-tropical, too warm for him.
There isn't an iceberg, snow drift or glacier.
No decent tundra, just lawns and azalea.
At least leopard seals are not too abundant,
sentry duty and lookouts quite redundant.
Of late he's been wistful and heaving deep sighs,
a faraway, unhappy look in his eyes
Is he the victim of an internet troll?
Is that why he's asking, "Which way's the South Pole?"

Thinking Without Trace

I read "The Life of Wendy Cope."
It sparks a flame. It gives me hope.
A bubble forms above my head :
"A Guardian profile double spread!"

I view my life through microscope,
an introspective slippery slope,
some episodes best left unsaid.
I'll grab another hour in bed.

Perhaps inverted telescope
would lend enchantment. Mustn't mope
nor dwell on childhood joys long fled.
I'll dress and help to bake the bread.

My verse embrace a broader scope?
Use wit and paradox and trope?
Do more to maximise street cred?
"We're out of flour, you silly Ned!"

Think thoughts so deep for bathyscope
and half-invented words I'll grope,
thumb lexicon from A to Z,
but first to "t'Tesco's mill" I'll tread.

Some depths to probe with stethoscope:
M/s-ogenist or misanthrope?
I whip up rhymes inside my head,
then whip the double cream instead.

Seen through retrospectoscope
a rosier tint assumes my "soap."
With seconds savoured, onwards sped,
I potter in the potting shed...

With panic seized, these lines I'll shred.
I've lost the plot. I've lost the thread.
I stand more chance of being pope
than emulating Wendy Cope!

The Reverend Pheasant

In place of congregation, there's a flock of errant sheep
who by and large ignore him. It's enough to make him
weep.
The Reverend Pheasant tries his best to make these
sinners rue
their misdeeds and their trespasses, then move to
pastures new.

He struts towards those gathered in waistcoat mottled
brown
with cheeks suffused a florid red, he looks them up and
down.
Smart feathers flap behind him. His dog collar's pristine
white.
He searches for a choice of phrase will make them see
the light.

His patience stretched and short-lived, ill-temper's in
his eye.
They must repent by August or they all will surely die.
"Stand up. Stand up for Jesus. Come back into the fold.
The Shepherd's good. He loves you," the Reverend bird
cajoled.

But sheep are sheep and just like sheep they need a lead
to follow
and "Lamb of God Redeemer," they found too hard to
swallow.
The Reverend Pheasant gave a shrug and left them to
their fate.
The sheep chewed cud, but took the time to slowly
ruminate.

Whizz Odd of Oz

Had Einstein been an Aussie,
he'd have shaved that dill moustache.
He'd have called Mossbauer "Mossie"
and played tennis with Pat Cash.

Had Albert been an Aussie
'E would not have mc^2.
He'd have worn a swimming cossie
and have surfed with Logie Baird.

He'd have been a Sydneysider,
Melbourne Mexican, Taswegian,
Alice Springer, Whitsuntider.
Possibilities are legion.

Had he been from Thursday Island
or Cape York's peninsula tip,
he'd have held the moral highland
and found some other salient quip.

There'd be no wave mechanics
bar the ones on Bondi beach.
Would this cause widespread panics ?
"No," said Schrödinger to Nietzsche.

But in far Ulm was Albert born
with no chance of being an Aussie,
unless amidst our alien corn
he'd lived. So he wasn't, was he ?

The Jewel in the Town

Blackpool's home to "Kiss Me Quick" and Albert
caged with lion,
but we take off for Scarborough, Yorkshire's Mecca-
Zion.
The sun shines bright. The traffic crawls. The miles
seem to expand
till we join "La Comédie Humaine" staying at The
Grand.

Imposing gem, lost Belle Epoque, fat tourists stand and
gawk,
its cornices and ledges echoing round to sea gulls'
squawk.
What! A bouncer on the front door, our room key his
demand;
times change when "La Comédie Humaine" is booked
in at The Grand.

We troop down to the dining room through ornate
vaulted arch,
meandering stream of paying guests, expectantly we
march.
But when dinner's served, the food is mass-produced
and bland.
These days it's "La Comédie Humaine" dining at The
Grand.

Postprandial stroll along the front, passed fifties' rock revival,
all sideburns, quiffs and blue suede shoes, they wait for stars' arrival.
Johnny Leyton takes us back with a doowop and roll band,
but today "La Comédie Humaine" is playing at The Grand.

The sea is ink. The heavens are lit by a single star,
whilst arcades flash their tawdry ads across the bay and bar.
An orange lantern moon climbs up, beam rippling to the sand,
lost on "La Comédie Humaine" at play beneath The Grand.

The ballroom's closed for changes, but the concert hall is packed.
The bingo caller's night is young. Her voice seems old and cracked.
At the SJT, Gilbert's Pirates pour sherry on the strand,
meanwhile it's "La Comédie Humaine" playing at The Grand.

And up the coast, where Whitby lies, the whaling fleet's left port,
bleached bones the only evidence to witness all they caught.
We drive by Whitby's floral clock (tea time by the hour hand ?)
but for "La Comédie Humaine", Time's over at The Grand.

And in their bedroom basement depths, false window on the wall,
staring out at solid brick, each couple awaits the call
from grim Honoré de Balzac. A pen glides in his hand.
Finis. "La Comédie Humaine" has booked out of The Grand.

Coincidence

We were gathered round the table at Macc's "Amuse Café."
The excuse we had was flimsy, not World Cup, not D-Day,
no big deal, just Food4Macc volunteers socialising.
French onion soup I'd supped (yum! yum!), then something surprising.
For main I'd chosen fresh fish cakes and when the dish appeared,
they'd served it on the Macc Express. That's when it all went weird.

Don't worry, friends, my seafood was not contaminated.
This was mere facsimile and semi-laminated.
The chef had wished to recreate, as in the days of yore,
that wrapped-in-newspaper effect, we had at chippy door.
It's pretty much extinct now, but for my generation,
fish and chips and printer's ink: instant salivation.

Now, as I munched my tasty choice, revealing inch by
inch
the photo on that front page, it made me kind of flinch,
for Jake, my step-son's mate it was, whose face was
grinning back,
a local rock musician, work well-known outside of
Macc.
A tad coincidental as I think you might admit.
It could have gone to anyone, but here's the spooky bit.

Jake's Dad's a dead keen cyclist, my next door
neighbour and a friend
and we'd just ridden on our bikes Great Britain End to
End.
For fourteen days we'd pedalled and for fourteen nights
we'd snored.
"Here he goes again," you sigh. "Re-cycling stories
make us bored."
So here's the point I'm making and though you might
boo and hiss,
when struck by one coincidence, how many do we
miss?

Dog or Cat?

Our Rob is miffed. He's in a mood.
"Are all you poets just mad or rude?"
And "Why is this?" we calmly ask.
Will someone brave address this task?

He says we never hymn the praise
of puppies, bow-wows, dogs who laze
whilst over-jumped by quick, brown fox
or greyhound racing from its box.

We do not eulogise the doggie,
but dedicate our "Odes to Moggie."
There's tripe like "Identity Kit-ten."
Even Eliot, TS, was smitten.

He wrote "Old Possum's Book Of Cats,"
dubbed "Practical," but feline brats
according to our expert Rob
who swears that every cat's a yob.

Salman Rushdie's "Sat On It Verses"
he hasn't read. He thinks it nurses
at its core (and he can't bear it)
curled up cats. He just won't wear it,

says, "Give me verse about alsatians
and I'll give you standing ovations.
Let me hear your 'To A Setter,'
then you'll hear me say, 'That's better!'

You can stick your puss and feline.
For the dog, I make a D-line.
Give me a lick from faithful mutt.
I'm one big, soppy canine nut."

It's strange, for Rob, you'll all concur,
knows how to make his audience purr.
When he's up there, a head of steam,
reading his poems, we're cats with cream.

The Yellow Orrell

Its yellow frame is blemished and great paint chips mar
the fork.
The lurid tales that bike would tell if only it could talk.
It's been brought in, neglected and stayed dirty, wet and
soiled
and left that way for ages when I know it should be
oiled.

It's crying out for TLC to clean away the dirt
with cloth which masqueraded once as my old briefs or
shirt.
Its cogs have teeth need scrubbing with a cast off, worn
tooth brush,
but somehow as its owner, I'm for ever in a rush.

So, Bike, be patient with me and I swear I'll change my
ways.
It just won't be this minute, but maybe, one of these
days...

LEJOG: Before

It feels like a grand slam when you've managed to bid
it.
At John O' Groats, here we are. We actually did it!
Fourteen days in the saddle, so we're tired and we're
sore,
but that's almost forgotten. What a great feeling!
Phwoar!
Nothing much here to relish, just the sea and some
gulls.
All those road miles on two wheels perhaps senses
dulls,
It's no Taj Mahal, not Ayres Rock nor Antarctic,
but now that we've finished, it's somehow cathartic.
Why don't we just turn round and bike back to Land's
End?
You cannot be serious. Are you crazy, my friend?

LEJOG: After

Our fourteen days have whizzed right past.
Our fourteenth home from home at last.
Wry smiles our mixed emotions hide.
Could we be planning our next ride?

Work

The month of February's renowned
for lovers' trysts, St. Valentine's,
when secret passions may be crowned
and pledges made: "Will you be mine?"s.

And while you yearn and heave those sighs,
admire her nose, her every quirk,
toast with champagne those sapphire eyes,
there's someone here who has to work.

Of course they say that love is blind.
It's sometimes deaf and often stupid.
For me, this is my daily grind.
I'm Eros, also known as Cupid.

My arrows pierce each lover's heart
seven twenty-fours, three-sixty-fives.
One guess who guides each winging dart,
till swains are husbands, girlfriends wives.

So gaze into those limpid pools,
write sonnets to her perfect lips,
but far too soon that ardour cools
as she puts weight on round the hips.

I've busy days, but 14th Feb
is just another working day.
Demands on me don't seem to ebb,
yet no-one talks of double pay.

Withdraw my labour? One of love?
You have your union. I have mine.
And when at last push comes to shove,
I'll be there for your Valentine.

Mm-Mid-Summer Sunnet

Wasps come tumbling drunk from the sun ripe plums.
Once the green, round fruit shows soft and yellow,
they make a bee-line for the laden tree.
They have no thought to share with you and me
as lazily we sip our wine, get mellow,
whilst somewhere, far away, the summer hums.

And how this June for once our senses numbs
with sultry, pulsing heat, not stormy bellow
nor beating rain: a month with pedigree.
It smiled just now on Diamond Jubilee
and shines from cover page of Time and Hello!,
which, as we doze, slide gently from our thumbs.

Tennis soon; sweet strawberries in a punnet.
Sunset glows on mm-midsummer sunnet.

Nightmare Too: The Site Race (with apologies to
WS Gilbert)

You wake up with a shock, cast a glance at the clock
and think of the task that's awaiting you.
It's the day of the race. In your throat there's a trace of
a ticklish cough aggravating you.
You go downstairs to eat English breakfast (complete),
know there's adequate time for digestion
and mentally prepare for the wing and the prayer of
which precedent says it's a question.

The morning starts slowly. It's suddenly wholly a blur in
your mind looking back at it,
then the time comes to change, your race plan
rearrange: Give best shot? Just get round? Have a crack
at it?
You warm up and canter, share jokes and the banter.
Almost everyone's humming and harring.
This is called "psych-ing" out; it's what racing's about.
It's all part of traditional sparring.

The list may seem endless. You're totally friendless; all
around you, pulled hamstrings and muscles,
groin strains, torn ligaments, mostly just "fig-a-ments"
conjured up by the forthcoming tussles.
Then it's up to the start, quaking nerves, pounding
heart. (It's adrenalin first that gets racing.)
Clear your lungs with a cough. In two ticks it's the off;
then it's you *v* the course that you're facing.

Some words from the starter, advice, a race charter:
"Marker ribbons always keep to your left.
Please take care not to fall. A good race to you all."
Then you're off as of senses bereft.
In a flurry of feet, just behind the elite, past the diner-
spectators in Mereview,
in the chaotic surge, you give in to the urge to keep one
eye on Rachel Pleeth's rear view.

There's shoving and milling. You nearly go spilling,
miss a bath in the Mere by a whisker.
You emerge from the straight, *(that's the part that you
hate)*, realise that the pace is still brisker.
So you've set off too fast, sense the others ease past and
your breathing is starting to labour.
There's no strength in your thighs and it's no great
surprise, there's a stitch in your side like a sabre.

You plunge into the mire, unlike "Chariots of Fire"
where the circuit's a cloistered quadrangle.
To say it's soft going is no way of showing what is felt
from the sufferer's angle.
You pass the first marshal. He's highly impartial. As
you near, he calls out your position
and he offers each one a Welsh phrase to push on,
though you'd rather he called a physician.

Having toiled up the crest, you ease back, take a rest,
then come round the first pool in a loop
and you know with that rise comes the part you despise, the
middle race where you're destined to droop.
You go into a trance. You've no drugs to enhance the
performance your body's demanding.
You just have this mission, vivid premonition of
fulfilling a role that's outstanding.

And you suddenly feel that your dream's become real as
you glide smoothly past the race leaders,
though you don't front the pack, since *they're* on their
way back and you're a mile adrift of the bleeders!
So, it's head down and work. Richard Hunt and George
Kirk are the ones who are destined for glory,
whilst grafters and toilers and middle-aged pot-boilers
aim to finish a quite different story.

There's a figure of eight where you go through a gate
(*it's the part of the race you're not keen on*),
then you leave CTL with its slopes up from Hell and
whose gates you were tempted to lean on.
You plunge down through the trees, make the most of
the screes till the mud all your worst fears surpasses
and you're back to the lake, though each stride that you
take is like freeing yourself from molasses.

As you round the last bend, you catch sight of the end
as of light from a far distant planet.
If you put on a spurt, ignored how much it hurt, you
might even be glad that you ran it.

So you're in quite a state, try to accelerate.
There's fire in your belly, but your legs turn to jelly,
all trembling and flaccid (excess lactic acid),
but you're catching up fast, though you'll never get past,
and your hotly pursued, mutter words which are rude,
though you've scarcely the breath for you're dying a
death
and is that death's rattle or part of the battle?
In your ears there's a roar which you try to ignore
and your eyes over glaze. All around you is haze.
Your vision is misted, both feet sore and blistered...

With a burst of elation, an eerie sensation, you come
into the straight on a PB,
but just as you thought that it wasn't for naught and
that one day you'll represent GB,
within sight of the line, you spy Hilary Fine, with her
helpers and friends to support her,
but there's many a slip for you suddenly trip and plunge
head over heels in the water.

You cough and you splutter. A camera's shutter records
the event for posterity,
whilst you contemplate the cruel hand of Fate, the
hours training, the days of austerity.

Then you wake with a fright, realise it's still night and,
like sunrise, the truth's quickly dawning,
It's a nightmare, a dream, an unconsciousness stream,
and the race doesn't start till this morning.

End of Season Rites

Early November and the greenhouse glass drips with
condensation.
"Sunbabies" dangle, little yellow baubles on their vines,
still somehow bringing sweetness and a touch of colour,
a foretaste of the festivities to come.
Flower pots, in disarray under the potting bench,
tumble together like the discarded leaves outside.
Soil-caked, half-forgotten tools prepare to hibernate
and I'm alone with the mature, yellowing plants,
alone except for snails, munching, munching,
munching,
but the sound I hear is Winter creeping across the plot,
stalking the last of the lettuce,
making the cream cones of parsnip syrup sweet.

I watch the sun setting above the far townscape.
It glints wanly on the slate roofs and aerials below,
but turns the clouds the reds of holly berries,
of "Gardener's Delight" and that cheeky, perching
robin.
Head cocked, is he singing for me?
Or for his young long flown the nest?
Or to charm those juicy worms from their clay domain,
a year's end feast to take him through to better times?

Women:
1. Cleopatra

Where desert sands kissed pyramids, the Nile caressed the Sphinx
and Cleopatra's beauty shone, the crafty, little minx.
All rolled up in a carpet, she arrived at Caesar's door.
"O wise and mighty Caesar, we should mutually explore

the possible positions our two peoples could adopt.
We must have a tête-à-tête," then down on his couch she flopped.
Julius was a man like me, not immune to woman's wiles.
Their son they called Caesarion and Cleo was all smiles.

Later with Mark Antony, facts which History underpins,
Cleopatra had three children, one son and boy-girl twins.
All would not end happily. With Mark Antony's last gasp,
Cleopatra too would end it all and snake to bosom clasp.

Women:
2. Boadicea/Boudicca

When I was growing up, she was known as "Boadicea,"
a wild, amazing Amazon brandishing a spear.
She led a tribe from Norfolk, the fearsome, bold Iceni.
Now I learn that much has changed since I was teeny-
weeny.

"Queen Boudicca: that's with two Cs," cry the
cognoscenti.
(Luckily for all of us they are around in plenty.)
In her chariot Queen B it was challenged Roman
honour,
but the struggle was in vain when legions set upon her.

The Romans were outnumbered, but they managed to
defeat
Queen B and the Iceni at the Battle of Watling Street.
Had Suetonius and his army failed in their aim,
the Romans would have quit these shores. Nothing
would be the same.

Women:
3. Jeanne d'Arc

A simple shepherdess, Jeanne d'Arc,
heard saintly voices, lit the spark
which saw the Dauphin crowned in Reims.
A bas les anglais! Vive la France!

The siege of Orléans was raised
and France's enemies were dazed,
but as she made the English quake,
they took revenge and no mistake.

In Rouen she was put on trial.
They found her guilty, used their guile
and in the flames she agonised,
but very soon was canonised.

Women:
4. Elizabeth I

The House of Tudor on the throne, Elizabeth was
queen,
but France and Spain were uppity, so Liz vented her
spleen
and went to war with them. By some curious
circumstances,
she routed Spain, but Calais lost, so all of France was
France's.

She may have singed Felipe's beard and repelled the
Armada,
but beating pesky Frenchmen, it turned out was even
harder.
Liz became embittered, couldn't bring herself to
Raleigh.
"Open up this feeble chest. On my heart engraved is
'Calais'."

Women:
5. Queen Anne

The House of Stuart ended with a Queen whose name
was Anne.
It started with James I (or VI) who clearly was a man.
The handover to Hanover went without a hitch.
Said George I, "Mein Gott, the Dummkðpfe. It makes
me want to twitch.

Mit Schottland they've united. Great Britain's one big
region.
I struggle mit King's English. Wie kann Ich face
Glaswegian?"
Three hundred years have now passed since the passing
of Queen Anne
and there's a move afoot to fox her not-so-cunning
plan.

Now, let me see. How does this work? The English
want home rule?
And leave the Scots out in the cold? They wouldnae be
so cruel.
Scots could not have our Head of State. The pound
would not be theirs,
but they'd be more than welcome to all our Tony Blairs.

Pollytricks

There are unpleasant noisy flocks,
a most annoying breed.
They rule the roost and strut like cocks:
the pits we're all agreed.

They sport red, yellow, blue or green,
the colours of macaw,
or even somewhere in between.
They squabble tooth and claw.

Birds of a feather the country serve
selflessly on missions.
Caught in full flight, they'll spin and swerve
our "party poli-, party poli-, party politicians."

If they have their plumage ruffled,
just listen to them squawk,
commonsense obscured and muffled.
My, how they talk the talk.

When in full flight, unstoppable,
you'd like to see them off.
They're even quite "uncoppable"
when caught with beaks in trough.

And hollow phrases they rotate,
streetwise and patrician,
but direct question answered straight?
Not "party poli-, party poli-, party politician."

No Robin Day or Paxman J
can knock them off their perch.
Babbling on, they have their say:
sometimes, "Bring back the birch;"

sometimes it's "Scroungers we will fix;"
or "Big Society,"
whilst revelling in their "politricks"
and impropriety.

To get your vote, they'll parrot guff.
They'll cash for questions take,
but all *our* cutbacks aren't enough.
Transparency's opaque.

To clip the wings of party hack
and curb his vile ambitions,
let's corporal punishment bring back
for "party poli-, party poli-, party politicians."

Winter

Incey Wincey's cobweb's decked with dew drops.
Holly berries glisten in the sun.
Winter corn shoots hint at next year's wheat crops.
Last year's race is very nearly run.

A bullfinch couple, perching, raid the feeder,
shedding sunflower kernels on the snow,
whilst grey squirrel, that pesky little bleeder,
stuffs his cheeks and dominates the show.

Meanwhile, the robin preens his ruddy breast plate,
from stroppy blackbird filches fallen grain.
He knows that solstice short days will not wait
and senses there may be the threat of rain.

The last of Nature's rubies cling to apple.
Willow herbs still have a seed or two.
The wizened leaves on trees, too few to dapple;
yet Winter sun, too feeble, can't peek through.

I trace the patterns on the snow imprinted,
ephemeral, and by morning gone.
Though sadly at Life's transience this has hinted,
these memories recall that sun once shone.

Personalised Number Poets

You'll have seen them with their flash verse,
souped up adjectives firing on all syllables,
tuned to perfection, yet built to last.
The lines are honed and glistening and so waxed
and polished you can see their reflections.
The body of work is trim, streamlined, frictionless and
smooth
and gets them where they want to go.
Not even air could resist.

Open up the verse. Have a look under the sonnet.
See how it works, what makes it tick,
what fuel-for-thought-injection systems are on display:
the twin verbs; the alliteration; all iteration.
What ingenuity has been involved in the design,
the economy of space, ergonomic perfection!

The same goes for the interior.
The choice of ancillaries is to-die-for,
whether you're talking vintage and classical,
all mahogany dash and sleek upholstery
or off the wall, post-modern, foot down, feet up,
the latest model, un-rapped, unprecedented,
first off the production line.

Listen to it go from purr to scream
as it races from iambic pentameter
to rap and back in seconds.

Take the convertible: a few deft touches
and it's a breath of fresh air.
The 4 x 4 performs on any quatrain.
The Poets Lorry-ate, with their big, butt of sack
payload,
now have a ten year tenure.
There's the family saloon: almost pejorative,
every day verse that we're all familiar with, perhaps,
but when you need to get from A to B (or not to be)
there's no question. It's no blur in the mind.
It's reliable and always there for you.
Good mileage, as driven by the B412D himself.
Yes, those personalised plates:

J K3475 in a fruity, mellow Autumn Mist;
TEN150N, a supercharged Light Brigade;
B7120N driving a Chillon Castle;
HA12DY T, out in all Weathers;
the old Clock Stopper himself, AUD3N;
HUG1-large screw-13S, no E-by gum-type;
and Burns, TamTam O' Shanter sat knav-ishly perched,
rides his M(e)G with RAB813 B plates.

WH17MAN, E2RA P and EL107,
are the American big three.
For 51MON A, there's the Range Rover 2010;
and for MOT10N, an Oxford Academic.

G120UND-breaking, EAR7H-shaking, BRE47H-
taking:
PLA73-tectonics.

Ghost Writers in the Sky

A Fleet Street hack was **writin' on** one dark and windy
day.
Upon his desk he rested as he wrote to earn his pay,
when all at once he paused and heard the **sound of
Johnny Cash,**
streamin' through his Spotify® which caused his teeth to
gnash.

The words were still on fire and the lyrics made him
reel,
of which footballer to write for and how to seal that
deal.
A bolt of fear went through him as books thundered
off the press
for he saw ghost writers comin' hard and that put him
under stress:

Plenty I owe, ohh, ohh. Plenty they pay, ay, ay.
Ghost Writers in the sky.

Their faces gaunt, their eyes were blurred,
their shirts were soaked with sweat.
He's writin' hard to catch those turds,
but he ain't caught them yet,
'cos they got to write forever for best sellers in the sky
with critics snortin' fire. As they write on, hear their
cries.

As the writers loped on by him, he heard one call his
name,
"If you wanna save your soul from hell in this our
writin' game,

then journo' change your ways today or with us you will write,
tryin' to catch the public mood into that endless night."

Plenty I owe, ohh, ohh. Plenty they pay, ay, ay.
Ghost Writers in the sky.
Ghost Writers in the sky.
Ghost Writers in the sky.

Wham, Bam, Thank You, Slam.

Coming to Buxton is always a blast,
though sometimes we find that the food isn't fast.
The "Cat and Fiddle" will serve until eight,
but Leslie and Rob are unlikely to wait.
The Buckingham's laid off its catering staff
and you can't really dine at just any old caff
when you're taking part in a Word Wizard slam,
especially when lunch was a salad of ham,
a mere distant memory, the calories burnt.
It's happened before. You'd have thought we'd have learnt.

The upside, the great thing, is just being here:
(though between you and me, there's also the beer)
the chance to perform, or in my case, recite,
a handful of poems far into the night;
to listen to others, feel their emotions
from peak dizzy heights to the depths of the oceans;
the suspenseful tingle as each round begins;
 and who gives a toss as to which poet wins.

Well, I do a bit, so this verse sycophant's
aim is to woo you if you think I am pants.

Emily

Emily's family is fearful and fretful.
She's advanced in years and becoming forgetful.
She lives all alone now her hubby has gone,
has acquaintance aplenty, close friends, just Yvonne.

She goes into town where she shops at the market.
If she came in by car, then where did she park it?
Or perhaps she just walked in... or was it by bus?
When they say that they're worried, they're making a
fuss.

At home, she's a menace and often in danger.
She'll open her door and let in any stranger
and twice she's been robbed of her pension by callers,
opportunistic, low life creepie crawlers.

Her fridge is packed full of her favourite meals,
but she'll half fill her trolley with two-for-one deals.
Most days she will need to be prompted to eat.
She won't know if she's hungry, nods off in her seat

or three times in one morning, she'll microwave soup,
let it go cold, reheat it, go through the same hoop
and sometimes it's still there untouched in her bowl
when she goes in the garden for her evening stroll.

The cooker's electric. They've cut off the gas,
a precaution for fear of what might come to pass
should she wish to ward off the nocturnal chill.
It's not she's defaulted and can't pay her bill,

but she might get distracted, blow her kitchen sky high.
Her neighbours are watchful. She thinks that they pry.
She's so mistrustful she has paranoia
and thinks that the world is there to annoy her.

She can't recall names and seems purposely vague.
They worry she's part of the Alzheimer's plague,
yet her eyes come alive and the words start to flow
when she starts recalling events long ago:

childish pranks with her cousins - she names every
one -
how poor, but how happy and how the sun shone;
how winters were snow-filled and magic back then,
as she slips into winter of old age again.

James Kennally-Smith

"Is that your gardener?" He turned to you and asked
as I was potting up down on our patio.
His dry, deadpan demeanour kept concealed and
masked
if he was teasing you a tad and in the know.

I missed the radiant, enigmatic smile you flashed,
which lies somewhere between BB and Jeanne Moreau.
Like Jules, or maybe Jim, I'm easily abashed,
but popped my head around the door and said, "Hello!"

"Come in, old chap!", exuding confidence, he chimed,
that confidence which comes with having lots of
dough.
The ritual of shaking hands we pantomimed
though, later, true affection from these seeds would
grow,

whilst you and I, snug in our am'rous status quo
have watched the years pass by and love come dropping
slow.

Nostalgia for Our Future

On the banks of the Guadalquivir,
where the murky waters rush,
hemmed into channels by mills which turn no more,
where Roman bridge joins mosque and tower,
she came towards me, as I lay,
flotsam washed up by another lunch.
Tall, with short-cropped hair, tanned and mystical,
a presence from another world,
peering into the setting sun,
upon the parapet above, she
lingered.

I gazed, admired, relished the fleeting glimpses
of our present through half-closed eyes,
drowsily devoured the fading visions of our future.
For us the gulf would not be bridged,
no lightning spark between our outstretched hands.
Like the otter's head - or water-rat's -
which broke the surface, bobbed and disappeared once
more,
she clambered back, rejoined her man,
disgruntled, out-of-sorts, was playfully rejected,
embraced, and, like our stillborn future,
vanished.

Four Characters in Search of Another

1. Character One

My Dad believed you could read at a glance
a person's character just from his stance.
Your spine like a ramrod with shoulders held back
meant you were the kind who might earn a blue plaque.
Yet he spent his days crouched up at the face,
round-shouldered and hunched up. There wasn't the
space.

He'd been in the Guards and the King's colours
trooped,
then Bevan's boys joined as our war fortunes drooped.
His Grenadier's badge on lapel he sported,
the clip below that the club he supported,
all working class, pigeon-fancying men
who sent their birds north to race home again.

"Sit up straight," he'd say as I slumped in my chair
and, "Get to the barber's. You've collar-length hair."
He'd use the words dilatory, rammel and piffle.
He'd no time for Elvis, Cliff, Dylan or skiffle.
And I sometimes remember now that he's gone,
his pet phrase was this: "Put first number one."

Yet he must have helped me to be what I am:
a poet; a gardener; a man who makes jam;
a cycling recyclist with a wry sense of humour;
who makes people laugh, at least that's the rumour;
a hoarder of stuff who's late to a fault.
Am I the cellar in which Dad put the salt?

2. Character Two

When "Bread Roundsman Acts Out of Character,"
appeared in one of the local papers,
it referred to me brother's Friday night out
and me Mam had an attack of the vapours.

He was always a bit of a tearaway.
He would stay out until one with his mates
and there'd be a big row between him and me Dad
whilst me poor old Mam it was arbitrates.

He was one of the last to be called up,
but he opted out to go down the mine.
Three weeks later, he joined the Artillery
hoping a military life would be fine.

He was sent overseas to Malaysia
to fight the MNLA communist threat.
He'd wade through rivers right up to his waist
in search of an enemy he'd never met.

One night whilst he was on duty, his mates
borrowed a jeep for a jape and then crashed.
So they all spent a spell in the slammer.
You might say his army career had been trashed.

He was later dishonourably discharged:
the worst soldier his officer had had.
With an ex-Grenadier Guard in the family,
well, imagine how it went down with me Dad.

So we're back to the bread roundsman's character.
In Malaya, our soldiers were tops, the bee's knees.
Back home, he's had a few beers and decides
the evening would end in the local Chinese.

When you're pissed, you've a strange sense of humour,
and when they tried to leave without paying,
a swarm of kitchen staff emerged with big sticks
and insisted the clients were staying.

And the rest, as they say, is His Story.
He was prosecuted, convicted and fined,
and "Bread Roundsman Acts Out of Character"
was from then on the way that he was defined.

Now I forget how long it was after
that he decided that he'd earn his crust
as a miner again for the rest of his life,
like me Dad, in his mouth the taste of coal dust.

3. Character Three

Don't get me wrong. My sister has character, too.
How could she have survived without some feigned
disguise.
 "She kept in control of her feelings all the way
through,"
said me Mam. "It's hard to be strong when someone
close dies.

She didn't make a fuss. I was so proud of her.
She gritted her teeth and made sure she got through it.
Never showed us all up by breaking down. No, sir.
She showed some real backbone. Well, that's how I
view it."

Sandy was fifteen, more like going on twenty.
Her first and last boy friend, was not quite twenty one.
Before them a future with promise aplenty
till that summer's day on the bike. Now they are gone,

on a long bend not cambered, just minutes from home,
holding waist tightly, with wind wildly caressing,
knotting and tangling tresses that wouldn't need comb.
We play the scene over, just wond'ring and guessing.

"Shall I tell them?" I heard me Mam say to me Dad
when I called as we set off to pick up our kid.
I fretted over news which could only be bad,
saying nothing and keeping my feelings well hid.

That's what we are good at, 'cos we're made of stern
stuff.
It was guilty relief to find that my daughter
was out of harm's way, safe and sound. Fate's "Blind
Man's Buff"
random spin has some living longer, some shorter.

4. Character Four

My Mum was christened Lucy Brown,
but she would sometimes play the clown,
adopt a pseudonym outlandish,
her alter ego's name she'd brandish:
Lucy Araminta Wilhelmine.
(Think Rose becoming Eglantine.)

It gave her style. It gave her standing.
It made her sound aloof, commanding,
perhaps a tiny bit Germanic,
less unromantically Britannic,
less common place, less working class,
more from the top drawer, more top brass.

It was our family's standing joke.
My Dad, an ordinary bloke,
a working man, no airs and graces,
with pigeon hat and belt and braces,
didn't go in for such pretences,
had no time for Marks and Spencer.

When pushed, he was a Woolworth's man
or Co-op with its divvy plan.
Keep it simple and keep it plain.
Owt else went right against the grain.
My Mum was sugar: sweet, refined,
when "Araminta Wilhelmine"-d.

But then again she had the brain.
She passed the scholarship in vain.
Gran would not accept charity,
aware of costs, disparity.
Mum's lot was mending stocking seams.
She'd just be fancy in her dreams.

Injury Time

1914

"It'll be all over by Christmas," they said,
not knowing the countless horrors ahead
and the dead
                    and the dead
                              and the dead
                                        and the dead...

Heartbreak Hotel Haiku

Roy knew from Elvis:
single man on double bed;
only the lonely.

No Regrets Haiku

It's no use crying
over spilt infinitives.
To boldly go then?

Post-Laborem

Nothing in his work
became him like the leaving it; retired
as one that had studied his retirement,
to paraphrase the thane of Cawdor's death
in what's referred to as the Scottish play.

True he did not shirk
and whilst VR was quite like being fired,
yet volunteers were a strict requirement.
His career's a ghost like Banquo's in *Macbeth*.
It matters not whilst bank has monthly pay.

Fireworks

All bangs, crackles,
dazzling explosions, fizzles.
Gunpowder!

Happily ignite jumping-jacks.
Kiddies leap, mothers nervous,
old people

quietly remembering sparkler trails.
Unbeatable variations.
Whoosh!

X-box®, you're zapped!

Acknowledgements

Sincere thanks are due to so many.

Top of the list is Mady who does her best to keep me fed and watered.

Over the last five years, Macclesfield Creative Writing Group has consistently supported, encouraged and egged me on and our workshops have provided many of the ideas which have found themselves on to these pages. Various other poems were specially written for themes dreamt up by Jude D'Souza for the fortnightly open mike, "Speakeasy", at the Snow Goose, Macclesfield.

Charlie Heathcote has taken valuable time off from recounting the activities of "Our Doris" to ensure that files got uploaded and Patrick Prinsloo has read proofs and given invaluable editorial advice when he should have been concentrating on nursing his hip. Thanks also to MCWG's Margaret Holbrook, Sandy Milsom and Joy Winkler *inter alia.*

The cover illustration of my parents is by the talented Karen Ross. The photo of an "Old Man with Wine Bottles" was taken by Phil Walker on my Real Men's Club* retirement walk in July, 2007.

Finally, thanks to all the characters who people these ramblings.

"Lunch Chez Simone (and Léo)" was commended in the Segora Poetry competition, 2015.

*strictly ironic.

Separate tables: Photographs by George and Jenkins, Mansfield.

Top half: Jean, Alan, Dad (Vernon) and Mam (Lucy) in foreground facing the camera at the wedding of John Burton and Doris Dickman, early 1950s.

Bottom half: the author, far right.

Made in the USA
Charleston, SC
13 June 2016